How To Sell Everyday In 3 Easy Steps

Deepaq V Vartak

Copyright © 2018 Deepaq V Vartak

All rights reserved.

ISBN: 9781730988394
ISBN-18:

DEDICATION

This book is dedicated to you and each and every sales person and business owner who get out of the comforts of their homes and go out to sell and make their customer's life easy by providing solutions.
This book is an attempt to empower you with the best sales skills and to help you achieve greater success.

This book is dedicated to every single person who I have worked with, my customers, my seniors, my subordinates and my colleagues. They all have made huge contributions in my life and hence I could process this book.

This book is dedicated to my family and friends who have always stood by me.

This book is dedicated to the divine force that always guides me and keeps me focused towards my goals.

CONTENTS

	Acknowledgments	I
1	Selling Skills. Why Do I Need Them	1
2	Purpose	5
3	The Sales Process	7
4	Sourcing	12
5	Connect	23
6	Serve	37
7	Sales Management	56
8	Buying Signals	63
9	Probing Skills And Consultative Selling	66
10	Selling To Investors & Venture Capitalists	73

Workbook of Master Sales System Attached

ACKNOWLEDGMENTS

I acknowledge with joy and pleasure:

My mentors and leaders with whom I had the opportunity to work, learn and master my skills.

My many trainees and students who encouraged me to put it down in a book for their and others benefit.

My many clients and business associates who have always kept their faith in me and my methods.

My family and friends who have been with me for last so many years as a great support and source of my strength.

1 SELLING SKILLS. WHY DO I NEED THEM?

If you are generating revenue for your organization, you are always employable. Isn't it true? And what better way to be in that position, than directly be in a sales function? Do you think selling skills are required only for people in sales function? Or should we say in every walk of life, these sales skills are going to help you to get better deal?

For example, if you are appearing for an interview, aren't you selling yourself? If you want to get married or start dating, don't you exhibit your unique selling points? If you want to start a business, don't you sell your ideas to investors, your partners, your employees?

When you are in midst of some negotiations you need excellent negotiation skills, that is again a part of selling skills.

Want to get across your point in meetings…sell your idea?

Want to convince your parents, spouse, partner, children, friends for something…sell? Right?

So, if selling skills are so important in every walk of life, then why do we run away from this word "SELL"? Why we pretend not to sell?

Why we shoo away sales men?

Why we don't want to accept that every person in some or the other way is selling at some point of time, directly or indirectly?

So rather than resisting let's get in acceptance mode and learn the skills sets that are required to make us a better sales person who can succeed in any walk of life.

Are you the one who finds it difficult to communicate with people? Do you struggle to initiate talks with people? Are you uncomfortable in asking for help? Do you find it difficult to even introduce yourself? How many times since childhood did you want to talk to that particular girl or a boy but you couldn't muster courage to go ahead and talk?

Every single time you have held back yourself, you have lost an opportunity of life. You lost an opportunity to get the spouse/friend of your choice. You lost an opportunity to get introduced to some important people who would have made a difference to your personal as well as professional life.

Every time you have lost these opportunities, more and more you have been convinced that you are not made up for sales or rather you are an introvert. You have lost on confidence to talk in public. Are you aware how much damage you have already done to yourself?

Now you have even stopped taking chances thinking it's not your cup of tea. You are not made to do business. You are just an average person and have to live in a particular way. You cannot do business, etc etc etc…

It's never too late. If you implement even 5 percent of what you learn from this self-help book, you will see yourself a very different person.

Selling skills are not only for sales people. Every person who aspires to do well professionally and personally will need these skills set almost every day.

Over the years, I have come across several such instances and as we progress, I will be sharing a lot of examples that will help you understand my point.

One of my clients was from tier 3 city in Maharashtra, never really exposed to the outer world. He was good in his work. He was a proprietor of a small scale engineering firm, manufacturing machines. He was happy doing that but at the same time had given up hope of multiplying his business after a few failed attempts and losing some money.

He did a crash course with him on selling skills and equipped him with the required skills set and what followed next was life changing for him. Within three months he started manufacturing machines for companies in other states of India. Within a year, he started supplying machines to Asian countries and there is no looking back now.

He learned, to think like a champion. He had gained in confidence that he can overcome any situation as he learned the art of selling and acquiring business, be it locally or internationally.

There are several such people who are stuck up in life at some point or another. All they need to do is ask for help and it is available. So never be shy to ask and you shall receive.

So this book is not only for sales person, but anybody and everybody can take advantage of the skills that you acquire through this book and use it in your day to day life and be successful.

A good sales person always gets away from any situation as he is coached to look for solutions rather than keep focusing on a problem.

You can master the art of selling as it is very easy. But as any new skill has to be practiced, this will need to be practiced too. With practice it will become a habit and then it will come naturally to you.

So, enjoy this book and make an attempt to learn as we progress. I have included lot of techniques and tools. Feel free to use whichever you are comfortable using.

Remember one thing, "It's not products that sell, people do". People buy People, always remember that.

2 PURPOSE

Whatever you do in life, it is important that you have a strong purpose behind it. If you have decided to be in sales or business then identify a strong purpose behind it.

A strong purpose behind your goals will help you to be on track all the time. You will have your ups and downs but a strong purpose will keep you focussed towards your goals.

If you read autobiographies of successful, you will realise all successful people had strong purpose statements in their lives.

Have a strong higher purpose behind your goals. If you want to buy that new house or new car, ask yourself, why you really want it? What is the real purpose behind it? Is it only to look good and impress upon your friends? Or is it that you want to do it for your parents and your family. You want to give them the best.

Why you want to succeed in your business, just to make millions or you want to leave a legacy for your future generation? You want to earn wealth to enjoy as well as help the needy ones and do your best that you can for them? Do you want to only splurge your wealth or want to put it to use by helping others as well?

Bigger the purpose in your life, there are larger chances of you enjoying your success. It also depends on how badly you want to achieve your goals. Once your purpose is defined, then you will know how badly you want to achieve that goal.

I come across hundreds of people having everything but still searching for something that they don't know. That's because they had not identified their purpose in life.

Your purpose for achieving your goals will come from within and on your mental makeup since childhood. Introspect and ask yourself, and you shall get the answers. Be truthful to yourself.

Once you have identified your real higher purpose of achieving your goals then write it down and keep it alive in your mind. This will help you to enjoy your success as well as the journey.

3 THE SALES PROCESS: IN 3 EASY STEPS

However talented you might be, if you follow the process, you get faster and assured results. You can't go wrong if you follow a time tested and successful structure in your learning phase.

How many times have you seen average or below average people reaching their goals or sitting at enviable positions? That's because they don't try and invent the wheel. They just follow the process and achieve their goals.

Similarly if you follow "The Sales Process", be rest assured of mastering the art of selling. Nothing can stop you from making a sale, however big product or situation it be. Whatever the product, be it any industry, "The Sales Process" will always be the same. Just apply it and get your results. Be it pitching your business opportunity to venture capitalists, pitching your product to your customer, selling yourself during the interview process or be it that appraisal time of the year or any situation, the process will be more or less same.

So what this sales process? It has been simplified to a **THREE STEP PROCESS… SOURCE- CONNECT- SERVE.** If you follow this three steps in sales or business development you will always achieve success. I will help you understand this in detail shortly but before we proceed further make sure you remember these basic.

SOURCE CONNECT SERVE - This simply means source new people to meet every day. During your interaction, genuinely connect with them. And Make sure you serve them well and take care of them. These are not just prospects or clients but your future customers.

As we move further, I will take you through the entire sales process step by step. But before you learn those steps, I want you to understand the concept behind The Sales Process.

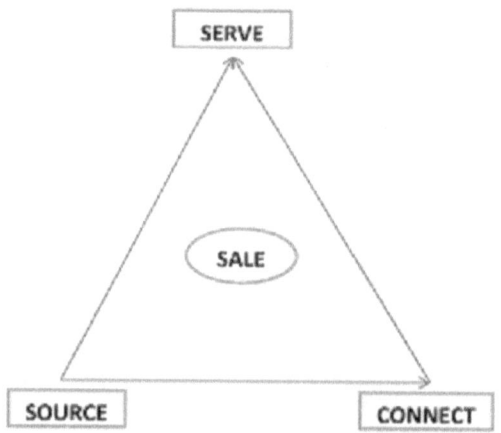

Let me give you an insight in what is sourcing...

"It was a lazy afternoon in Goa. I was driving back from one of the sales calls with my team member. Goa sleeps in afternoon, so the roads were practically empty and we were in interiors of Goa where generally only selective tourist go. While I was enjoying the lovely road surrounding with all green trees around and in midst having a healthy chat with my team member, all of a sudden I noticed a latest model black Mercedes was speeding towards us from opposite direction. It crossed us quickly and I noticed a Goa number plate on it. Within a fraction of second I decided to follow the car. I quickly took a U-turn on that narrow road while my team member was asking what are we doing? I told him I could smell new business in that direction and so we are following that Mercedes. I don't know what he must have thought at that moment, but he really did not had any choice. The black Mercedes was nowhere to be seen. We were driving like crazy but just couldn't locate it. Further down the road, my team member spotted the car parked in one of the building's open garage which was not easily visible. We decided to do a quick Reece. There was a small food joint close by. We went there and ordered two cups of tea. Yes it was painful to have tea in Goa but I was there for business, you see. Well, in Goa people are generally friendly to tourist. And we could make out that the guy was himself the owner of that food joint. We started a friendly discussion with him. Within no time he shared with us the name of the owner of the Mercedes car and about his business but he could not help us with the telephone number. I asked my team member to go and check if there was any business sign board and see if any phone number is mentioned. As luck favours the brave, there was a business sign board and a phone number written on it. The rest is history. We managed to sell him three insurance policies with Rs. 5,00,000/- lac premium each within two months." Well that's called prospecting or sourcing a prospect. And all the business commissions went to my team member's account and he can't thank me enough even today. Even now after so many years when he calls me, he remembers that experience and since then he has never looked back in his career.

In short, you have to be always sourcing and alert in sales.

Each of the steps mentioned above will lead to business.

These are very powerful and effective steps. Success is almost guaranteed if you follow this sales process.

To help you further understand the process, I have split it further down

Sourcing
Prospecting
Planning

Connect
Meeting & Greeting
Rapport Building
Strong Opening
Identifying Buying Motive

Serve
Need Analysis/ Need Creation
Product Presentation
Objection Handling
Closing
Customer Delight

It is important to have a complete buying on this sales process. If you follow this process every time, you will get results every time. It is as simple as that.

The general thumb rule in Sales is 1:5 or 1:10 (Sales Closing ratio) depending on the industry that you are working in. But during my many years of experience, I have experienced many a times 1:3 to 1:1 sales closing ratios just by following this process.

Many people, whom I have trained, have experienced such high closing rates by following this sales process.

This means that your rejection ratio is drastically cut down by following this process.

Your success ratio and sales closing go up dramatically having direct impact on your revenue generation and target achievement.

4 SOURCING

Prospecting & Planning

Prospecting

Tell me honestly, how many times in a week or month do you have this question in mornings, "Whom do I meet today for a Business/Sales Call?" Every sales person or entrepreneur who is looking to source clients, faces this question, isn't it?

This is not a right situation to be in. To be successful in sales and business development it is utmost important to have appointments at least one week in advance. You need to know how many people you are going to meet over next week.

Depending upon your profile and business needs you need to know that how many NEW sales/business calls you need to have every day. Yes it is NEW calls that matters, you may have number of follow up business calls to do, but doing new calls is the key. And new calls have to be done every day.

Yes I understand your challenges. Most of you have already exhausted your list of contacts within first six months, you don't have many phone numbers to dial to. So what can be done?

I will share number of ways to build up your new business call list on a regular basis. You can choose which methods suit you. I suggest you try various things and see which is generating maximum new leads for you and stick to it. But it is always better to simultaneously keep doing other activities as well.

If you are able to understand exactly what I want you to do in prospecting, that alone will increase your business at least five times if not more. Yes I am serious and I mean business. This is the key to your success. Over the years I have always come across sales people who are so predictable in their sales numbers and they take pride in it. That's fine, but if your numbers are not growing sizably, then you are not making money or earning your incentives. What's the point in doing only that is expected? If you follow the principles given in this book, nobody can stop you from making money at least five times more than you are making at the moment.

Choose Right Segment

The reason most people fail in sales because they are not willing to go out of their comfort zone. They are very cosy in targeting the segment where they come from or the segment one level below.

I will share one real life case to help you understand what I mean. This is when I was working with one of the life insurance companies. One evening, one life insurance agent came to me and was sharing how her commissions were almost static since one year that she had joined and that was not sufficient for her to take care of her expenses and so wanted to leave the life insurance industry. After doing a detailed analysis of her performance with her and her manager, I gave her a new corrective action plan. Simultaneously, asked her manager to provide her the required training and support for next few days. The next time she met me was almost after eight weeks or so. Even today I can't forget that day. She was so delighted and wanted to thank me for my time and the inputs that I had given her. Her commission cheques just started to multiply within first 4 weeks. Her average case size went up considerably. She started to up sell quite often to same customers. As a result her commissions almost doubled up within six to eight weeks.

All I did was, I corrected her target segment. All these months she had been working really hard in meeting people who had limited resources of finances to buy her insurance policies. They would buy the least possible amount at the most and so she never made much in commissions even after working so hard. I asked her to trust me and asked her to start targeting clients in higher income segment. The problem was she was never comfortable meeting those people, but the reality was, that is where the money was and once we trained her to cater to that segment, she started making almost double the commissions in equal amount of time. That's the beauty.

I have seen almost 90% of sales personnel with this problem. They are happy to source business from their comfort zone market and so their results are mediocre or average, but far lesser than what they are really capable. What's the point in catering to the market segment where there is limited money or resources? Just change your target segment to higher income group and see the dramatic changes that will start to happen. All of a sudden, you will start closing higher ticket value sales. You will cut deals much faster and make much more money in the end. I have helped so many people multiply their sales and income just by changing their target segment and the results are very fast.

It is not at all difficult to go to higher target segment.
Well, if you really want to succeed in your business or job, at some point in life you will have to learn to go to this segment. This is where the resources are. More than anything else, it is a question of your mind-set. Most of you don't really want to

come out of your comfort zone. You are fine meeting same kind of people rather than upgrading yourself and targeting clients in higher segment.

Train yourself, and just go to this higher target segment. So how do you reach this segment? Most of you will already have this question. Well, during my training sessions, I spend good amount of time to helping change your mind set in shifting to higher target segment. It appears easy to say just leave your comfort zone and put yourself in a uncomfortable situation, but it is the most difficult part to do it practically. Even experienced guys get stuck up at times and are unable to change the scenario.

This requires mental toughness and some discipline. You need to have that kind of confidence in you to go to that higher segment for business. And confidence will come from practice and product knowledge. You need to know your stuff, then nothing can stop you. You need to know your product or your business thoroughly. You must know everything that can come up during a business call. So being prepared is half the job done. You need to know about your competitors products as well. This will give you edge in the market place and you will never shy away from going out and meeting people in any segment.

It's okay to fail. Initial business calls might be tough on you if you are naive and underprepared. But the key is to never give up.
You must have the courage to pick up that phone and fix your appointments and go out and meet people. Successful business people, always have phone numbers to make business calls. They are never lost in the mornings on what to do today. It requires practice and discipline too.

It requires mental toughness to accept rejections. Most people shy away from leaving their comfort zone because they are scared to take rejections. Most people just cannot handle rejections. They tend to take rejections personally and hence they are not able to make new contacts and pitch their business to variety of people who are out there waiting for them.

Always remember " SW SW SW SW SW". This means " *SOME WILL, SOME WONT, SO WHAT, SOMEWHERE SOMEONE IS WAITING*".

This should be your life mantra when it comes to meeting new people for business.

Art Of Referencing

Other important aspect of successful sales professional is that they always take reference. Retrospect yourself. How many times do you do it as a habit? You will get the answer. Every business call you make, you should have this goal that you will never come empty handed. You will either sell or at the least, come out with minimum three references from every business call. You should be aware that it is much easier to close referral calls than cold business calls.

The conversion percentage is almost 80% higher as compared to cold business calls.

Then why most of you never seek references from your clients? I will help you answer that.

To ask references, you must have followed the "Sales Process" correctly. And if you have followed your sales process correctly, most often you will get business and if not business, then at least references to call for next day. If you have done your business call as per the process, it is your right to ask for business and references. But that confidence comes only if you have done the call correctly and you would know it immediately.

You must be disciplined enough to never leave client's place before you have collected references. This way you will always have sufficient number of business phone calls to make for next day. And the best part is, when you are working in that higher target segment, these people have high credibility and chances of closing these sales calls magnifies. Secondly, the references also come from higher target segment as these people move around with same kind of people.

So henceforth, make sure your sales call ends with business or reference, either of it is a successful business call.

Activities For Generating References
I am sure, most of you must have done some kind of activity to generate sales leads. Few of you must be still doing at times. But the success lies in doing it on a regular basis.

Depending up on your business needs you must plan at least one Activity per month or per quarter. You decide what suits best for you but this has to happen.

Benefits Of Doing Lead Generation Activities
1.   You can reach the Target Segment where you want to focus on by doing an activity directly in that segment.

For example: If you are selling only to CEO's and all C-suites category people then you need to do an activity where these people meet. So you must be updated with the kind of seminars that are happening around the city for these CEOs etc. and make sure you attend those.

Once you visit such seminars, summits and meetings, make sure you also look one of them. Move around and exchange your card with maximum number of people. Don't just jump from one person to another. Be polite, be helpful to them, offer to help, do everything you can and get maximum leads. Alternatively you can even get the entire guest list with email addresses and cell phone numbers and use it. There are many ways to do it. See which fits you and just do it.

2. Other benefit of doing a lead generation activity is that you will always have a lot of numbers to call up on.

3. When you are making that phone call for meeting, most of the times people have met you earlier and exchanged cards or shared their details with you, so easy to get their time for appointment.

4. With more number of activities, you become known in your field. People start associating you with the services that you offer. You will be surprised but it's true. You become a known figure and you start getting leads with ease.

So now just don't sit and wait for things to happen. Go out and do the lead generation activities.

Some of the activities that you can do for Sourcing
1. Attend Club Meetings, join some clubs, attend seminars, etc.
2. Most common ones are doing drawing competitions in residential societies, schools etc. or a quiz
3. Arrange blood donation camps
4. Arrange free medical camps etc.
5. You will be surprised but let me share this activity with you. I am from Mumbai and had done this in my earlier days. In Mumbai we have those "Pan walas" and "Chai Walas" where all sorts of people stop over for a smoke and a cutting chai.

What I used to do is select a right area where there are lot of corporate offices and then go and meet the "pan wala" or "Chai wala". Ask them to collect visiting cards from their customers with some incentive (eg. One Hall's toffee free if they drop a card).

By evening I used to have more than hundred cards collected. All quality leads. You can incentivize the "panwala" or "chaiwala" for better cooperation. Amazing isn't it?

You can try it out and see the results.

6. You can make use of social media sites to get in touch with people. Sites like LinkedIn and Facebook are used to increase contact list. Be creative in your approach. Don't be me too types.

7. Carpet scanning is another successful lead generation activity.

There are several lead generation activities that you can do depending on what you are comfortable with and your target segment.

Once you have adequate list, it's time to make that important phone call.
I have seen many sales people getting scared of that first phone call to the prospect.
The best thing to do is prepare a script and practice.
Sample script: " Good Morning Sir/Mam, I am (Your Name....) from (Your Company name...). Is this the right time to talk to you?

If yes then proceed, or else ask if you can call back after couple of hours... If yes, then directly come to the point. Tell them what you have to offer. And ask when can the prospect give you time.

Ask close ended questions so that you are in control of the call. Otherwise the prospect will take you for a long ride and it will be a waste of time.

Examples of Close ended question:
a. "Sir, would it be fine if I call you back by 4 pm?"
b. "Sir how are you placed tomorrow first half, between 11 am to 1 pm?"

Please note that answers to above question will be direct yes

or no. No beating around the bush business.
This will come by practice.

Key is to keep calling prospects till you don't get the desired number of appointments for the week. Hence make sure you always have more than enough number of phone numbers to get sufficient appointments.

Once you have enough number of meetings then hurray…
You are on your way to make those important sales calls.

Planning
Before you go out on field and meet your prospect, it is important to do proper planning for the call and also plan your day correctly.

Planning for next day has to be done in the evening and NOT on the same day morning as most of the sales people do.

For a field sales person, the most important part of the day is tour plan.
Make sure you have planned your route according to your appointments and you don't end up travelling to same place several times of the day and waste lot of time in travelling. This has to be taken care while you are arranging your appointments. Meetings in same and nearby areas have to be finished when you are in that area. This way you will get a lot of time on hand for better working.

Plan your strategies for each call well in advance. Pack all the necessary information that you have to give to your prospect/client the next day. Do not put it for next day morning.

This will not take more than ten minutes of your time. Planning is key to complete all your appointments on time.

With better planning you will realize that you are always on time for your meetings. This is important as I have seen so many people losing out on business only because they were not able to reach on time for their meetings. Most clients take your punctuality as an important yardstick to measure your professionalism. So make it a habit to reach on or before time.

Successful sales people go on step further. They even plan what they are going to wear the next day, well in advance.

Other important aspect of planning is continuity of a sales call.

I always tell my trainees to have a continuity in your sales calls. For example, if during your last call, the prospect had asked you to come with some extra proposal, pricing or for that matter anything that you had promised, then make sure you remember that and carry it in your bag during the next call and hand it to him immediately. This will help him recollect last discussion and you can start from where you had left last time.

This is one of the very important part of the sales process.

Benefits of planning

1. You are well in control of your day, this helps you to be confident and relaxed and you go about doing your work effortlessly

2. You are most likely to complete all your appointments

3. During the sales call, you are totally ready with your material and everything else that you might need.

4. Good planning reflects in your sales calls and your client/prospect realizes that he would like to do business with a professional and dedicated person like you.

Planning Checklist

1. Have you planned adequate number of calls for the next day

2. Have you planned your route correctly

3. Have you planned your inputs and material for each call

4. Check for continuity from last call and carry if anything you need to carry as per your last meeting with the client.

Congratulations. You are all set on go on field next day.

5 CONNECT

Connect is a small word, but it can take you long way in life.

Connect is the second part of our sales process structure. Connect is also the most important part of our sales process structure.

It's important to connect to your prospective client before you attempt to make a sale.

You will be surprised to know that in initial few minutes of seeing you or your interaction, the prospective client had already unknowingly decided whether he will buy from you or not. Rest of the call depends up on these initial few minutes.

Most of the modern day sales persons skip this step conveniently and straight away try to sell. Result is rejection, under sale or a sour relationship and a lost client. That's the reason you see a lot of client retention problems with current businesses.

If you are able to connect to your client then you will have him all your life. That's a guarantee.

So what is this 'connect' and how to connect is the question.

If you are genuine and client's interest is top most on your mind then you will by default connect or make an attempt to connect with him.

You will be able to empathise, care and provide a genuine solution to client's problems.

Once you genuinely empathise and put yourself in the client's shoes, you will immediately connect with the client.

You will learn to put client interest above your sales target and your company interest. Trust me friends, you will only sell more by doing this. Take my word for it.

For some people it comes naturally and some of you will have to make a an effort to master the art of Connecting. Once you start practising, it will become your habit and over a period of time this will become your nature. Your nature to care for your clients is very important. This will bring you a lot of success in sales and business.

The steps involved in Creating a Connect with your prospective clients

1. Research Through Social Media before meeting them/ OR by using your Observation Skills when you are at their place for meeting (Can be a part of planning)
2. By correct way for Meeting and Greeting them
3. By building Rapport
4. By Identifying their Buying Motive
5. Strong Opening

Let us understand above steps in detail

1. Research Through Social Media before meeting them/ OR by using your Observation Skills when you are at their place for meeting

Let me share my real life incident of gathering information on social media site.

I was given an appointment by my "Inside sales" team member. The client was a successful businessman and well connected.

I went to his profile which was well guarded so not much information was available on it. However I stumbled upon a very simple information that he had a dog of a particular breed.

That was enough for me. Rather than doing further research on my prospect I did a quick ten min research about the breed etc.

As usual I reached for my meeting well in time. Was offered coffee and was waiting for the client to see me.

Once I entered his cabin, after exchanging initial greetings, I linked my discussion to his dog. And we ended up talking about his dog entire evening, how his dog grew up and then his share of health problems etc.

Before I entered his cabin I never knew him, but we were chatting like old friends. Trust me we discussed the product only for five minutes. Not a single minute more. And I walked away with the contract.

I was able to connect with him. And I was genuine. If you are genuine, it shows up. You need not make an attempt to look genuine.

With advent of social media this has become really easy for all of us in today's times to have at least some information about our prospective client before we meet him.

This does not mean you have to stalk the client. You are advised to maintain this decorum and respect client's personal life.

Things you should look for at their LinkedIn, Facebook, Twitter, Instagram etc. profiles are:

Which clubs they are attached to?
Their latest vacation or any other celebrations.
Their favourite books etc.

Any other interests.
A little information about their family.

All above information will help you to start the conversation. It is very important to talk to prospect about his interest etc. and build a rapport before you go on to business.

When you meet the prospect make sure you mention at some point of time that you have visited their social media and you gathered that particular information about him over there. Don't hide it from him. It is always important to speak truth and be genuine during your sales call and otherwise also.

Most clients appreciate that you are going extra mile to understand him and help him decide.
These small things go a long way in building rapport with the client.

Observation:
When you are at the clients office or house for a meeting keep your eyes and ears open. You can get a lot of information about your prospect there.
One of my prospect had a lot of trophies and certificates displayed on his wall and in his cabin.
All I did was just ask about his achievements, what made him so successful, how he keeps himself motivated etc. We connected and I got the business. Simple isn't it?
Yes. Selling is simple if you follow the process. That's why at the beginning I have said that "products never sell, people do".
People want to do business with people who they think understand them. With little effort from you, you should be able to do it.

2. **Correct way Of Meeting & Greeting Clients**

I have seen number of sales people doing some common

mistakes while meeting their clients.

A lot depends upon building your character in the eyes of the prospective client and meeting and greeting is one of them.

Things to do for effecting greeting

a.   Be enthusiastic about meeting the prospect. Your enthusiasm should be clearly visible in your body language and a twinkle in your eyes. Enthusiasm will add up to a very positive tone of your voice. If you are enthusiastic, then the entire vibrations in the room get changed. So make sure you are enthusiastic in meeting your prospect.

It doesn't matter if you are having a bad day or you are upset about something. Don't take it to the prospect and spoil your sales call.

It is your responsibility to start your sales call on a high and enthusiasm will help you in doing that.

b.   Have a firm handshake if offered. In some professions like pharmaceutical products selling where a sales representative meets the doctors, they don't offer a handshake , so make sure you are aware the norms of your industry before offering a handshake.

A firm handshake is a sign of a confident person. So take this opportunity to exhibit your confidence. I said firm handshake, not a very hard, hand-crushing handshake, okay?

c.   Smile. Most of you are aware that if you smile, the other person smiles back at you. So make sure you give a very pleasant smile to your prospect. Don't get intimidated by the stature of your clients. Just relax and smile.

d.   Greet the client as "Good Morning, afternoon or evening as per the time", smile, shake hand and wait for the response.

A very important advice to you all is NEVER ask your client or prospect "How are you?"

Because if your client is having a bad day and he starts it on a negative note then it becomes extremely challenging task for you to hear him out and then get him to listen to your product.

It's always a risk asking this question, hence the best it to avoid it.

e. Whether standing or sitting, make sure you have a good body posture. Be submissive in your body language.

f. Maintain a good eye contact. But make sure your eye contact is not intimidating.

After initial greetings let us move to our next step

3. Building Rapport

Why do you think building rapport is important? I had said in the beginning itself that "People Buy People". Yes however good product you may have or however talented you might be, if your prospective client doesn't like you then they will not do business with you.

Hence this step becomes very important ladder in the sales process. If you don't do this and directly go to your services and products, then chances are that you might face a lot of rejections.

So, how to build rapport? If you learn to build rapport quickly, then you should be able to connect with the client instantly.

The problem is that during a fresh sales call (face to face meeting is referred to as a sales call), you don't get much time to build rapport.

This is the usual complaint that I get from sales people when I coach them on this.

But actually that's not true.

You will have to remove that mental block right away. Before we move on how to build rapport, clear your mind of that myth.

Two important things to do while building rapport are:

First make an attempt to build rapport in every sales call

Second, with practice in first ten calls, it will become a habit, so do it until it becomes a natural habit to you.

With social media coming in, it has become quite easy in building rapport. You just have to go through your prospect's social media profiles and understand his interests, his latest updates etc.

When you go to clients place, start the topic positively, on his interests etc. and see how he starts speaking.

If you are genuine, you should be able to connect instantly. Please don't do it as a process. To be a successful sales person, you need to first be a good human being. As a good human, learn to take interest in others as well. Show genuine interest and see how well you will connect with your prospect.

If you are visiting their office or house, keep your eyes and ears open. Anything worth discussing, go ahead and discuss.

Some pointers to this are as below:

Many people display their achievements, certificates etc. in their office.

Their receptionist or secretary might reveal something latest about your prospect.

I have spoken to my clients on various subjects to build rapport, examples:

Vacation
Traffic
Weather
Cars
Sports bikes
Latest news
Sports
Food
New restaurant in client's neighbourhood
His style and choice of clothes, furniture, office ambience etc.
His Friends, colleagues (with Caution)
His watch
His fitness
His staff
Location of his house or office
And many more…

There are so many things. But make sure you pick up something positive and start only on a positive note. Never touch a negative discussion.

Stay away from religious and political discussions.

From now onwards, before every sales call, make sure you start this discussion with the intention of rapport building.

Only last year, I was at one of my prospects office. We were unable to meet as out timings were not matching and this went on for almost 6 months.

He is a successful businessman and a busy person with great clarity of thought.

Finally our timings matched and we decided to meet at his office. I was meeting him for first time. One of my existing client's had referred me to him.

Now, look at the real scenario. I had only 30 minutes. Thereafter he was to head home, pick up his bags and go to the airport. He was to go for an exhibition in Dubai.

I had this information as he had told me about this earlier. So what do I do? How do I talk on his interest and build rapport and then proceed further?

I will tell you exactly what I did. One day before the meeting, spent two hours on internet, took out all the information about that exhibition, past 3 years data of that exhibition as it was being held every year, the participating outlets and their exact locations, considering my prospects business I had done a strong research on every aspect of that exhibition and how his visit could be more fruitful and much more.

I had prepared a detailed report and handed him the file in the first minute of our meeting. I shared my views and insights with him.

After our meeting at his office for 30 minutes, he drove me to his house (his driver was driving my car and following us), we had early dinner at his house and then till the airport he was picking my brains on the exhibition and likely sales from it.

We ended up spending three hours and when he was back, we signed the contract.

So what is the learning in this for you?

Did you see, how soon I built rapport with my prospect. In fact with in first minute of our meeting I hit right notes and ended up spending three hours instead of 30 minute.

Thereafter, signing the contract was only a formality, as my prospect knew that if without hiring my services, I can be so much helpful then how much value I could bring in as a consultant.

Do you think we ever discussed product??

So my dear friends, no excuses on following the step of rapport building. This is the most important step and if done correctly, will really take you long way in your career.

Practice rapport building in every call.
Be genuine and take genuine interest in your prospects.

Identifying "The Buying Motive"

Now what is buying motive? This is very tricky and to be a good sales person you must learn this fast.

Buying motive is the real reason behind your prospect buying products.

Let me explain this by sharing a real life example.

In my early days as a representative, I use to meet doctors for promoting my company products. I had this habit of talking to my clients about other things than business before coming to my products etc.

One fine day before entering his clinic, I noticed a new luxury car in his parking lot instead of his usual car that he had been using.

On enquiring with his assistant, I got to know that he had just purchased that car two days ago.

I knew that I had got this excellent opportunity to speak on that car in that meeting. I congratulated the doctor for his new car and started to talk about its performance and brand value etc.

And what he said next really blew me up. He said that he had bought this luxury car only because the other doctor in their group had bought one a few weeks ago and how that doctor was showing off his possession. So to square him up, my client had gone and bought a higher variant of the car and have been showing it off to his doctor friend that he too can afford it.

Can you believe this? In short, the buying motive of my client was that he will buy anything if that helps him enlarge his image or brand equity or whatever you call it.

Once you get this important information then it is easier to push your products by matching it to his buying motive.

There are different types of buying motives with different types of people.

I will share a few reasons why people buy some products

Convenience

Performance/Efficiency

Safety Features

Appearance/Aesthetics

Economy

Pride/Pleasure

There can be many more. But these are the major ones that you must know.

You will learn to notice that some people buy products depending up on their budgets only. For some, it has to look good, for some people, it doesn't matter how much it costs or how it looks but it has to perform better. Some people buy only because it enhances their personality of just by possessing that product it gives them a ego boost.

Once you know what's the real buying motive of your prospects, then all you have to do it pitch it accordingly and close the sale.

Yes, it is as simple as that.

These are all finer aspects of sales and only few in the business would tell you all these techniques.

Look at yourself and introspect your buying motive. Recall the important products that you have bought in last 12 months and real reason for buying that particular product. You will notice that the buying motive has been constant in most cases. That's the reality.

You will learn to identify the buying motive of your clients with practice of asking right questions.

Once you probe them correctly only then you will know the real reason why they buy products.

Strong Opening

Once you have done all the above steps, it is very important to start your sales call with a strong opening.

What I mean by a strong opening is that the first sentence that you say about your product or services should start ringing bells in your prospects mind. It should grab his attention immediately. It has to be effective.

If you manage to do this, you will have his attention and you can do the rest of your call.

One of my managers had thought me to use a very different yet, effective call opening statement.
It said that " Sir, as you are aware, today Sachin Tendulkar is the No1 batsman in the world, similarly, my product _____ is the No1 in …………….."

Can it get any better? In those days Sachin Tendulkar was at his peak and his form made entire nation laugh or cry, feel great or feel bad. Just by using his name in call opening, I use to get entire attention of my client. That was the idea.

This is just one example and as I mastered the art of selling I started using so many innovative strong opening statements that my clients use to be totally with me during my sales calls.

Few examples that I used

"Sir, I have read, all self-made billionaires started with saving some part of their earnings, irrespective of their cash-flow. Similarly….."

"Sir, as India has a rich heritage and strong roots that keeps us grounded and focussed similarly…….."

There are many more, but I urge you to be creative and make

a few originals of your own. Use them in every call that you make. See the impact. Make it a habit.

6 SERVE

This is the Final step in our 3 step selling process

If we have done our earlier two steps correctly, then this step merely becomes a formality. But it is important for you to have a good helpful mind-set to be successful in sales for longer duration.

In this final step we will learn about

Need Analysis/ Need Creation
Product Presentation
Objection Handling
Closing

Need Analysis/ Need Creation

By now, you know a few things about your prospect. You have built rapport with him. You have done your preliminary homework before meeting him. You have identified the buying motive of your prospect. You have used strong opening statement to start your sales call.

Now next step is to identify a genuine need or create one.

My personal belief is that there is always a need and always money available to fulfil that need. But only that no one has ever told your prospect about his need. And if at all anyone has told about his need, the prospect must have given inadequate finances as the reason to stay away from fulfilling that need.

This is where you will be different. Equipped with all the knowledge about your prospect you must now start building your case for the product or services.

This has to be done by asking close ended questions. Close ended questions will always lead to 'YES' or 'NO' as answers. You will have to lead your prospect by asking these type of questions.

If you have built the rapport by now, then he will comfortably answer the questions.
If you have not done rapport building correctly then he will hesitate to answer. This will give you clear indication whether you have done rapport building correctly or not.

Rapport building is important step as by building rapport, you also build trust with your prospect. Trust is very important in doing business.
If you reflect in your past calls, you will understand now that why you have lost a few clients.

Rapport building opens up the client to speak up and share information about him to you. Your prospect starts to trust you as you have connected with him.

This helps you to identify the need for your product and lead the prospect in accepting it that there is a need for your product or services. This has to done by probing technique. By asking correct close ended questions you can lead him in accepting that there is a need for your product.

At every step, take his approval.

Now, there is a technique to ask these questions. First of all you will have to talk less. Allow the prospect to speak more.

Your sales call has to be a two way process.

I have seen so many sales persons, who will talk, talk and talk about their product and then wonder that why they have not made a sale.

They do believe in their product, work hard, do adequate sales calls but don't get desired results and then they think that sales is not a good career option and they leave.

It's not about you. It is about your prospect. So let him speak. The more he speaks up the closer you are to close the deal.

Once he starts speaking, ask neutral questions that will lead to the need for your product. Once that is started, ask leading close ended questions and let him arrive at a dead-end where only your product can help.

For example if you are selling financial products…

You – "Sir, would you agree that it is important to create assets for long term that would give you financial freedom?"

Prospect- "Yes"

You- "Great, sir, you will agree that a time required to create a good asset could be in a range 7 to 10 years or more"

Prospect – "Yes, depends"

You –"Thank you sir. As mentioned by you earlier, since you want to create asset for your daughter's foreign education which is likely to be in the same range of time horizon, would it be fine if I share a comprehensive plan with you that matches your need?"

Prospect – "Yes"

See, how smoothly you have taken his approval by asking leading close ended questions. Effortless, isn't it?

This is just one example. You can be creative and make your own question sets that will help you to lead your prospect where you want.

There are so many products and services and so many creative ways of asking close ended questions.

I recommend, you spend some time and make your own set of questions in the same fashion.
Ask this questions frequently so that you can master it.
Depending upon you product and services you must do need analysis and take prospects approval in various steps mentioned above.
This will give you firm footing for the next step.

Product Presentation

Since you have done need analysis and also taken your prospects permission to showcase your product or services, do full justice to it.

Don't be in a hurry. Follow the process. If you have visual aid, or product broachers, remove them a give a detailed presentation.

Don't just go through it. Glance at your prospect to see if he is with you and take his occasional approval.

Be thorough with the text or your product information. Make sure you are aware of the completion products as well.

Today, the clients are well informed as the information is available or a click of the mouse. So make sure that you are giving all genuine information about your product.

FABing

I am sure most of you are aware of it but still want to mention it.

FAB means,
Features
Advantages
Benefits

When you are talking about your product, don't just talk about features of your product.
Tell the prospect, what your product will do to hi. Talk about benefits.

Clients relate better to benefits rather than features.

For example
If you are selling to a doctor
Feature of your product might be
Sir this medicine has to be taken only once a day.

Don't stop by saying only this

Add further…
Sir since this medicine has to be taken only once a day, it is very convenient for your patients to take the medicine. They will not miss the dosage. This will lead to faster recovery of your patients. So apart from patient compliance it also offers efficacy.

Look at the difference in both the communications.

So every product you talk about to your clients, you must communicate what your product will do to him rather than only telling about what features your product has.

I have mentioned little more about FABing in Consultative Selling chapter

During presentations, if the prospect is not paying attention, stop. Resume only when he is back to you. He must listen to your presentation.

Speak clearly and communicate effectively.

Objection Handling

I have seen many experienced sales persons also dreading with objections raised by the clients.

Most sales people don't want clients to ask or raise objections.

I will tell you something very different.
You must wait for client to raise an objection. Because the moment objection is raised, you have an opportunity to CLOSE the sale.

Yes, objections are opportunities to close a sale.
Always remember this.

Sales people get irritated or even uncomfortable the moment objections are raised. This happens because of the mind-set and also the fact that they are not coached to handle client objections successfully.

Smart sales people want their prospects to ask questions and raise objections. Because they know that that is the opportunity to close sale once they successfully answer their objections.

Remember **NO OBJECTION = NO SALE**

To handle objections successfully, you must have complete product knowledge and also knowledge of competitor's products. Only then you will be able to handle objections and compare your product benefits to others.

There is a small process to handle objections successfully

LAPAC
Listen
Acknowledge
Probe
Answer
Confirm

The moment your prospect raises an objection, listen to him carefully.
Acknowledge him by saying 'Thank You Sir' for raising an objection.
If you have any doubts then probe him further with a question or two that why and from where this objection is coming.

Is it coming from past experiences? Is it coming from just listening to somebody?

Or it is just a genuine concern of his?

Once you are clear of the objection and its source, answer it in detail.

Once you have answered the objection, check with the client if he is satisfied with the answer? Have you answered his query correctly?

This is a very simple yet very effective process for handling objections.

Now, there can be different types of objections

False Objection/Stalling

This is the most common objection that comes up.

No money to buy or invest/ we will see etc… is a most common objection that comes up.

This is nothing but stalling.

If you have done all the steps in the sales process correctly then this objection can be blown off by doing benefit selling and offering various payment terms etc. in worst case scenario.

Other objections can be hidden objections. In this case the prospect is not very much willing to raise the objection.

This might happen if you have not done the sales process correctly. Hence he is hesitant to ask or raise objection. Other reason could be he may not have understood your product correctly.

To avoid this situation, make sure you follow the entire sales process correctly so that such a case doesn't arise.

Some objections are tricky in nature. In these cases prospect projects that he is with you and would give business but not now.

These types of clients are very smart and better salesmen than many sales people.

They will always keep you hopeful but never give business. Mostly these are the clients with whom you think you have developed excellent rapport and you are very friendly with them.

You have to be one step ahead with them. Once you know that any client falls in this category, you will have to show your clear intent and purpose of meeting him. Be little tough if required but don't allow such clients to take you for a ride.

Learn to deal with them.

Real Objections
Many a times your prospects have real objections. Such cases get closed immediate once you handle the objection successfully.

In all kind of situation, you have to follow the LAPAC process for objection handling. Most of the times you will get desired results.

Prospects, who may not give business, will end up giving at least references.

Remember, your prospect can raise objection any time. Even during your presentation. Make sure you make it a habit to handle the objection then and there.

I have seen many sales people not handling objection in

midst of their presentations and just continuing with their presentations. That is an insult to the client.

Closing

This is the most important part of our sales process and so many sales people are not comfortable with this step.

There is one inbuilt step in CLOSING, that is AFTB. AFTB means **ASK FOR THE BUSINESS**.

Once you have done all the steps in the sales process correctly, you have done your product presentation correctly, you have successfully handled your prospect's objection, then IT IS YOUR RIGHT TO ASK FOR THE BUSINESS.

Only sales persons who do not follow the correct sales process or fail to handle client objection, do not dare to ask for the business.

"ASK AND YOU SHALL GET". If you don't ask you will never get. Always ask for the business.

You need not wait till the end of the call. Anytime during your sales presentation if the client has raised an objection and you have successfully handled it, YOU HAVE THE RIGHT TO ASK FOR THE BUSINESS then and there itself, don't keep it till the end…

You will be surprised to see your closing rate dramatically going high.

And with the Closing Techniques that I will share with you, you will start closing sales calls more often and making a lot of money in commissions.

Successful Closing Techniques

1. **Direct Close**

To be used after product presentation. If objection has been raised by a prospect, and successfully handled by you, then immediately go for a close.

Examples
" Would you like to go ahead with this new product that serves your......., and helps you to........."

You can fill in as per your product segment and its benefits.

2. **The Summary Close**

Example

"Well Sir, this is the product that matches your requirements (narrate the requirement) and also fits in your budget. How about buying one today?"

3. **Third Party Close**

"Sir, this is just to share with you, Mr........... in your neighbourhood had similar inhibitions about trying our new range, but after using it he totally satisfied and now a regular customer of ours. Let us start with a initial order and see how you feel about it."

4. **Trial Basis Close**

"Well Sir, I can see you still have little inhibitions about using our range….., hence to help you to arrive at a decision, you can buy a trial pack with us. And once you are satisfied, you can place a regular order with us."

5. **The Alternative Option**

"Sir, which one would you like to buy? M500 or M750? Both will serve your purpose".

In this method you are not giving any other option to the prospect. This is very assertive closing.

6. **The Assumptive Close**

"Sir, considering your need and usage, I suggest you to go for this version….."

Now, after you have used any of these closing techniques, there are only three possible outcomes

Yes, I will buy it now.

No. I don't want to but now/I don't need it now.
Let me think.

In case of 'YES', just take out your order form and start filling and ask for the cheque number or payment method. Ask for references.

In case of 'NO', ask for references and don't leave without references (only if you have done all Sales Process Correctly), or else PROBE him further and understand the real reason and handle the correct objection and then close.

In case of 'LET ME THINK' there is one more final closing

technique called;

7. **The Build Up Close** Or Method Of **Continued Affirmation**

Immediately say "Sir thank you for giving a thought to my product/......."

"Sir, just to sum it up, you will agree that this suits your need of ...." Right sir?

"My product benefits of …….. & ……. Offer you.......", right sir?

"In that case, if this fulfils your need and also offers you benefits as good as these, then what's stopping you from taking a decision? Please let me know so that I can help."

If the prospect opens up and talks about limited finances, you know how to nail it. Either show your value proposition or offer payment plan and close the deal.

I am sharing three more powerful closing techniques, but I add a word of caution to it. Please use these techniques only if you are confident and totally in control of your sales call.

I have used these very often and my closing ration with these techniques has been 100%. That tell you how powerful these are.

8. **Half Nelson Technique**

When to use:

When a prospect is showing no interest/trust in your product or services.

When he says "I have seen many such products. They don't work etc."

How to use this:

"Sir, thank you for sharing your concern. Well if I show/prove it to you that my product has got all the features and benefits that you are looking at, gives value for money, and suits your exact needs, then in that case WILL YOU BUY MY PRODUCT TODAY?"

Rest is just a formality as you are confident of doing a strong presentation and after objection handling, sign him up.

Other powerful Closing Technique is:

9. **BULL's EYE**

When to use:

Can be used before you begin your sales presentation.

During rapport building if you have managed to get important information about what your prospect is looking for, then use this technique.

"Sir, if I am not mistaken, ... is this what you are looking for in a product?"

You have to hit the **bull's eye** in terms of his needs/ requirement/ wants.

If you manage to do that, he will jump out of his seat and hold your hand and say, yes man, you are right, this is exactly what I am looking for, do you have one?

Then position your product benefits accordingly and close it.

10. **Crawl-back Close**

WARNING: This technique is to be used only when over a period of time you have done everything in your control and you have tried all the closing techniques at various points and you have not got the desired result. Or else if you use this technique too early, you will be taken as a week person in the eyes of your prospect. So use this technique judiciously.

This technique is used in cases where you have been trying hard to convert a Super Smart Customer but he has not yet given you any business. There is a need, you have the product, you have done everything in your control yet failed to get business.

Mostly in cases where there is a Big Distributor, an Opinion Leader, Top COI (centre of influence), etc.

What You Say- "Sir, I need your guidance today. I will not speak to you about business today. But I want your invaluable feedback."

Sir, you are aware that I have done everything in my capacity to convince you to ....

I know you have the potential/need. I know I have the products range that matches your/your customers' needs. But still I have failed to convince you. I request you to help me in understanding what mistake I am doing so that in future I will learn to serve Top Distributor/ etc. etc. like you... Have I ever hurt you in any way?

Please tell me sir...

Invariably he will share the reason and that's your time to CRAWL-BACK in to close the sales call...

Thank him for sharing the reason and go for the close.

I am able to share all these precious information because, even though I had grown in the system and reached to top position in Sales Vertical, I never left going on the filed.

Somehow, I always found time to go with my subordinates on field and help them close sales. By doing this I have only added vast knowledge and rich experience to myself.

Sales is my passion and want to see all sales people successful.

Use all these methods and be a successful sales person

You have to master all these techniques and be prudent in using them. With practice you will succeed. I am confident that you will implement every word in this book. Even if you implement only 10% of knowledge, still you will multiply your sales. But my recommendation is make maximum use of these techniques.

Customer Delight

Last decade or so almost every company's focus has been customer delight. Earlier only a select few companies went that far, but with the increase in competition it has become inevitable.

The second most important thing about being customer focus is that it is directly related to repeat business. In most businesses, sixty percent of the business is repeat business. This in possible only if you keep your customer happy. Or else with so many choices available, your customer will be taken away swiftly by your competitors.

Then, how to give that customer delight to your clients? How to make them come to you again and again?

You have to go that extra mile to serve your customers. Hospitality industry is the best example to give for giving a great customer experience to its regular customers.

I know some top hotels know exactly what their regular clients want in their rooms. Their favourite flowers, fragrances, the way they like their breakfast and meal... Everything is noted and served every time the customer visits them. No doubt the customer feels at home and most importantly feels special and he wants to visit them quite often.

In your business you too can make a habit of giving your customers excellent experience.

Whatever you product or business, you must focus on doing that extra for your customer. And it doesn't really cost much. You need not spend any amount on it. A handwritten thank you card goes a long way in building trust and relationship with your customers.

With social media, it has become easy to know your customers likes and dislikes, their birthdays etc.

I know of so many successful life insurance agents worldwide who give top of the world experience to their clients and they know that it is because of this kind of treatment that they keep getting business from their customers.

Wish your customers on their birthdays, anniversaries and special occasions. Remember their choice of products and tastes.

You really have to make feel your customer like a king. So many restaurants offer free valet parking to their clients as a service, it really works for them.

This generation sales people, do business and forget their customer. And then they feel awkward to call them again for repeat business as after first sale they have never bothered to call or visit the customer. Do not do such mistakes.

Always visit your customer after the sale and enquire if he is happy with your product and service. Ask for references. Build trust and keep these customers for life.

See how you can make the process convenient for your customers to keep doing business with you. Simplify it for your customers. Your customers need to enjoy the experience of doing business with you.

Give them a WOW experience.

Never say no to your customer's special request. Always be accommodating. He will come back to you only for this purpose again and again.

Know what is important to your customer. Give it to him. Keep him for life. You focus should always be to serve. Business will happen, you need not worry about it.

Look at most of the top companies and brands nowadays. What they do? They offer loyalty programs, privilege programs and many such things to keep their regular customers interested and keep visiting them.

You can do your bit at your level. Nothing is small or big when it comes to customer delight. You have to try everything that you can think of and do it. Whatever brings smile on your customer's face and brings you repeat business, keep doing it.

Always make it a point to attend to customer complaints and disgruntled customers. They should make it to your priority list. I know owner of one finance company, who was struggling with generating new business. Later on he shifted his focus only on serving unhappy customers of competitors and he has made a fortune.

You too can do it. There is an opportunity in unhappy customer that you must tap. Be it yours or others customers, you solve their problems, serve them and keep them. They are s sitting gold mine with buying power. They have bought your or your competitor products and they can buy again. Make them happy and they are yours.

7 SALES MANAGEMENT

This is another important aspect of sales.

"Inspect what you expect"

If you are employed as a sales person in any organisation then I believe that you must be having some kind of sale management tools to monitor your activities and performance.

If you are an entrepreneur of a SME set up then there are chances that you may not be having advanced sales management tools.

In both the cases, you can use the tools that I mention below and be successful.

Why Sales Management Tools are important?

I personally know that most sales people don't like to do paper-work or admin work. They consider filling these data sheets and just an exercise. I know most sales people don't fill up all the data that they are supposed to. This also costs them dearly during their appraisals but still they don't learn.
It is all about their mind-set.

You have to understand that when you fill up your sales planning versus your actual field/sales activity, you create a lot of data that can be analysed and help you to get better in your game.

Data Speaks. Remember that. If you have done well, your data will speak and if you don't do well, your data will still speak. Analyse and learn from you data, take corrective steps and achieve your numbers.

Most sales people get defensive when asked about their sales call data. In fact you must carry it with pride and own it. I so often hear that there is pressure in sales job, but realistically speaking, if you are doing everyday what is to be done, then there is no relaxed job than a sales job. And no other job can be as satisfying as a sales job as you can gauge your success and failures very quickly.

You get to know your success and failures at the end of every day, every week, every month, every quarter and every year. This happens only in sales function, isn't it?

It's time that you change your mind-set on sales management tools.
Sales management tools are to support you to be on track and to monitor and analyse your performance. If implemented and analysed well, it can do wonders to your performance and learning.

Some must have Sales Management Tools are as below:
You can device your own excel sheets to capture and maintain data or use the one's that I have given. Idea is to capture this data on a daily basis and maintain record.

Once in every 15 days make it a habit to revisit your data and learn to analyse. You will be surprised to see how much your data can speak to you. It can give you volumes of information and insights.

1. Daily Call Report

2. Number Of Visits per month to your Prime Customers/Distributors

3. Number of Lead Generation Activities Planned and Conducted for the Month/Quarter.

I don't like to burden the sales team with too many data sheets. Just couple of excel sheets or your software that captures data easily should be fine. No duplication. Your core activity is sales and that is where you must spend most of your time and energy.

Data Analysis
Data analysis is an art and it is a must have skill for sales people, leaders, entrepreneurs, business owners and many others.

Daily Call Reports –
To be filled for Field sales calls. Many Tele-callers and inside sales teams also do maintain it.
Things you must capture in daily call report are as below:
Client Name
Contact Information
Agenda for the meeting and actual discussion
Total Number of meetings done for the day
Number of new clients met
Number of Sales Calls closed for the day
Frequency of client/distributor meeting (Means how many times you meet that particular client or distributor)

All these information has to be cumulative so that you get figures for Day, Week and Month as well.

Important pointer

You will notice that your business figures/ number of calls closed positively, is always directly proportion to number of sales calls done.

In short, when you do more number of sales calls, you tend to close more number of calls. This is always true.

The best time to enter your data in sales management tools is immediately after the call. If this is not possible then best is to do it on the same day, any time, even at night but not beyond that. If you keep it for next day, it becomes a habit and your data NEVER gets entered.

You also tend to forget a lot of important information and discussion that transpired during the sales call. In fact you lose up to 70% of the information that you were supposed to capture.

For a successful sales career it is important to maintain your data and also to analyse it regularly.

As you grow to the leadership position, you will know the importance of data and other sales management tools. But to get maximum benefit to you and your company, you should have the habit of doing it every day only then you will have the conviction of getting it done from your team.

Other important aspect of Sales Management is Reviews

Sales Reviews
"What gets measured gets done".

You must conduct minimum two reviews in a month.
Mid-month review and Monthly review.

I would like to share a few techniques here.

Whenever you are reviewing your team, make sure it is purely in excel format and not on presentations.

In presentations, I have seen people giving lot of stories and mentioning all unreasonable and unrealistic things as well.
But when you conduct sales reviews only in excel format, there is nothing to boast about. It's all numbers. It's targets versus achievement. It's about calls reports. It's about sufficient activities done or not done. No goof ups. Of course, you have to be wise enough to know the figures and catch the bluff masters, if any. But as it will become a habit, you will notice that your team will get a message that, you are serious about targets and achievements. You take sales reviews very seriously and you have total ownership on it.

You and your team will do everything to beat deadlines and achieve numbers. Within few weeks the scenario will change and you will notice that your team is totally aligned to you and your company goals.

Process of conducting Reviews

Ask questions.

Yes. Ask right questions. Make enquiries if there is a shortfall on number of business calls, activities or business figures.

You need not be aggressive but you need to mean business.
If the reasons are justified, take it up on you to support your team members either by joint field work or training support or product knowledge or whatever is needed to do.

If there are few people who don't want to change, get tough with them. But sales management has to be followed. This is one of the most important aspects of sales and sales leadership. The faster you master it, better for you.

Feedback
In a sales leadership role, your success will depend largely on sales management and feedback sharing.

During reviews, if you need to give feedback make sure you give it and don't hold back. It is important that the right message must go.

Performers should be openly appreciated and rewarded, but reprimand has to be in person, one to one discussion.

This will create mutual trust and respect between the leader and his team mates which very important to build a winning team.
There is a mechanism to be followed for sharing and seeking feedback.

Feedback has to be given to performers as well as non-performers.
Performer's work and results should be appreciated and rewarded. To get better at work, they should be encouraged to raise their bar and over achieve targets. They should be inspired to take additional responsibility of doing numbers and adequate support should be provided to help them achieve and be successful.

For non-performers, depending up on case to case basis, feedback should be shared and importance of achieving targets to be imbibed. Their inputs and activities should be monitored and help them to plan better strategies to achieve their goals.
Only if need be, do not hesitate to put them in performance improvement program. But the sole intention of putting them in PIP should be to help them achieve their business figures and make them successful. During PIP, it is the leader's

responsibility to help his people achieve numbers and come out of PIP successfully. That's the trait of a great sales leader.

A sign of a great sales person or a leader is that he is always aware of his numbers and statistics.

Whether in good times or even in bad times, they are aware of their numbers and this quality makes them distinct and stand out. Such sales people will be down for a very little time and they will bounce back for sure with tremendous performance.

8 BUYING SIGNALS

Successful sales professionals are super talented to pick up any buying signals from the prospect.

What are buying signals?

Any suggestions, information about his need, your product short comings etc. and any other information that can help you to understand the prospect and close the case can be considered as a **BUYING SIGNAL**.

Many serious buyers do often give these kinds of signals knowingly and unknowingly. Few trained sales professionals are quick to take the opportunity, do further probing, objection handling and close the call right away.

But most sales people fail to pick these buying signals.
I will help you understand how to pick these buying signals and increase your closing ratio dramatically.

Here is an example to help you understand.

Example 1.

Location: Mobile Phone Showroom

Salesman is explaining the features…

Prospect asks, "what's the battery life?"

Salesman answers and continues to tell about more features of that model.

The salesman has just lost an opportunity to close the sale then and there. The moment the prospect has asked him about the battery life, his next PROBING question should have been, "Sir, are you looking a Cell Phone with good/maximum battery life?"

Prospect - "Yes."

Salesman - "Thank you sir. Let me show you cell phone models that have the best battery life in its class" and goes on to show the specific models/features and closes the sale.

If you are selling a product that can be felt with the hands and if the customer picks up your product and feels it in front of you, that is a very strong buying signal. You must go for the close.

If the customer picks up your product brochure and starts reading it, that's a buying signal. This tells he is interested in buying your product.

During your product presentation/demonstration if the prospect asks for the price, that's a buying signal. Tell him the price and ask for mode of payment and close it. It can be as simple as that.

If the customer tells you that the price is not right, that's a buying signal. Either sell him the value proposition and if any room for negotiations and do it and close the sale.

9 PROBING AND CONSULTATIVE SELLING

Probing

In India, many car buyers don't drive their cars. They have chauffeurs to drive their cars. Not many car sellers ask this important question to their prospects, "Sir, do you drive your car or you have a driver?"

In most cases, the sales person will talk about performance, mileage etc. and waste valuable time.

A good sales person will ask him above question and then tell him that "since most of the times you are on backseat, look at the spacious legroom that this car offers". And go on to speak about the smooth ride and comfort that the car offers and close the sale.

This is called probing. Probing is asking right questions and many a times during the sales process asking leading question to the prospect that will help you sell and make him buy your product and services.

But how many sales people have courage to ask questions to your prospects. And even if you manage to ask, are you trained to ask correct questions? One wrong question and you are likely to lose a sale.

One incorrect way of asking the question and you hurt your prospect and hurt your chances of closing.

Many experienced sales people also dread from asking important questions to the prospects and hence not able to maximize the chance of closing.

Probing is necessary and most important part of consultative selling. But asking questions to your prospects can hurt you as many prospects have high egos and they don't want to reveal much information to you. Many a time it so happens that the information you are seeking is confidential and hence prospects are not willing to share it with you.

Let us learn the art of probing and consultative selling.
There are different types of question you ask prospect.

Open Ended Questions
Leading Questions
Close Ended Questions

Open Ended Questions
Open ended questions are asked to gain information, understand the needs of the client, to get desired information that you already know but want him to speak about and also to make the client talking.

What
When
Who
Where
How
Why

This kind of questions will help you gather the information that you need.

"Sir, what is your choice of molecule in treating patients with Lower Respiratory Tract Infections?"

"Sir, what is your dream vacation plan that you always wanted to make?"

"Sir, while buying a car, what the top most feature that you look for in the car?"

Above questions will do three things:

Give you client's Buying Motive
Give you adequate information to focus your sales pitch on
And make the client talking

Caution: WHY questions have to be asked with lot of caution. These are interrogatory questions and can hurt client's ego. You need to add a lot of cushioning to these kind of questions and should be mastered with practice.

Leading Questions

Leading questions are questions that lead the client in affirmation where you want to lead him. This is an art to take the client where you want to take him and he just follows with his own approval.

"Sir, I am sure, with good performance, you also look for good mileage in a car, isn't it?"

"Sir, while buying a smartphone, the most important feature that you will look for is battery life, isn't it? As if the battery is not going to last all day, then what's the point in having so many features that you may not be able to use otherwise?" Right sir?

Look at above questions. The sales person have actually led the client to accept his point and his focus area where he want to lead him. These are the strengths in his product and he will close the call effortlessly thereafter.

Leading questions give you complete control of a sales call. It is important that you are always in control of the call, and not the client.

Closed Ended Questions

Closed ended questions are asked to zero in or narrow down the problem area of your client.

"Doctor, do obese women have greater risk of infertility?"

Some super sales people would use close ended question in such a powerful way… But with practice it well before you use it…

"Sir, if I show you that this is a better plan for you and your family, would you like to buy it?"

After using above question, it is one hundred percent closed call.

You must write down or make a list of questions in above three categories as per your product benefits and practice.

It is important to have the wisdom when to use which kind of questions.

Generally at the beginning of the call, you make use of open ended questions to find facts and make the client talking.

In middle of the call, you make use of leading questions and once you sure of his needs, you zoom in with close ended questions and go for the close.

But it is at your discretion when to use which kind of questions depending on the stage and situation of your sales call.

Practice will help you to master the art of probing. This is a must have skill for consultative selling

Consultative Selling

Consultative selling is nothing but asking right kind of questions to understand facts and client's needs and then following the sales process that you have learned in earlier chapters. Top it up with probing skills that you have learned in this chapter.

Benefit selling and competitive selling is other aspect of consultative selling.

In benefit selling you must focus on benefits of your product rather than only features.

Every product has three components

Features
Advantages
Benefits

Most sales people tell about features and never sell benefits.

Feature is what your product has. Benefit is what your product does to your client.

When you start selling the benefits of your product to your client, your entire approach towards the sales call gets different. Your focus shifts from your product, to client's need and solution providing by selling the benefits that your product has to offer.

Extra battery life in a smartphone is a feature.

The advantage of extra battery life is that the user will be able to use the phone and talking time for longer time.

But the real benefit is that since the battery will last for longer time or for entire day, the user will not miss any business and personal calls. He will always be in touch with his near and dear ones.

And the most important part is that he will not lose any business in future, as now his clients can reach him all day long and he can do business deals well after office hours and during his travelling time. Isn't this a great benefit?

You have linked the benefits to his profits. He will buy your product.
Did you notice the big difference benefit selling offers?
Just telling a feature and selling a benefit a huge shift from a simple sales person to consultative sales person.

List down all the features, advantages and benefits that your product offers and start making use of it in every sales call and see the conversions happening.

Competitive Selling

To be successful big time in sales it is important to do competitive selling. For competitive selling you must be aware of competition and its products. You must know all the product feature, advantages and benefits of the competitor brand.

Most importantly you must know the short comings in the competitor's product and how your product scores over the competitor.

Yes having superior product helps but it is not necessary that only superior product sells. It is entirely on the sales person to make his product superior or inferior.

Competitive selling has to be done when you are sure that the client is using competition product and now you want to get entry in this market. You also need the share of his business and hence it is imperative to sell against the competition.

You can grow your market share by two ways, by capturing new markets and by selling to competitor's customers. In such case you need to have the skills to do competitive selling.

10 SELLING TO INVESTORS/VENTURE CAPITALISTS

This chapter is primarily for business owners and budding youngsters/ who have an idea and want to make it big.

Everybody who wishes to be rich, wealthy and financially free, will relate to this chapter quickly.

Has it happened to you that you know that you have a million dollar idea and if you get a right investor you would make it big?

As a small business owner how many times have you thought that I wish I had few extra money to pump in my business as I know this is the right time to invest and reap huge profits, but you were always struggling to manage that kind of capital?

Yes I understand you all have been in this situation many a times but have you done anything? If yes and failed, then congratulation as this is the first step, to go and approach investors

Let's get to the steps involved in selling your business idea to investors and venture capitalists.

Idea Conception
Preparing Project Report
Execution (In case of running business)
Fund Raising

Let us start with Step 1

Idea Conception
People, who are in thinking business, regularly get ideas, but some ideas stick to them for years together. They know it that the idea is great and it can change their fortunes but they don't take action on it due to lack of funds. Then some day they see that the idea is already taken by somebody else and that people are making huge profits and you say to yourself, "I wish I had the money or investors to finance my idea".

But the problem is you don't know how to sell your idea and you don't have the courage either to go to people.

So before you think of going to people to sell, gather all the courage you can and you need but dot it any ways. Just do it first 7 times and them you will be comfortable. It will be a new normal to you to go out and sell your ideas to people.

And with these steps it will be much easier for you to do it.
Once you have that million dollar idea write it down. Keep improvising on it till you can. Look around if there are any businesses with similar idea running and making profits. In my personal opinion it is absolutely ok to have similar ideas and businesses as long as all are making money. Why reinvent the wheel, if the idea is to make money.

But if you have a good idea that can be monetised for profits, that's great.

Write down your idea, make it better and better by thinking

about it. Visualise how you can implement it. List down all the challenges and limitations that come to your mind. Iron out the flaws that and fine tune your idea.

After doing this when you are finally convinced, that is the best idea you have got and it can be monetised for profits, freeze it.

Preparing a Project Report
Make a complete project report of your idea. Take professional help if required but get it done. It is most important. Because when you take professional help, there are so many other aspects that come up during project report stage that will compel you to think further and improve upon your idea. And trust me, it doesn't cost much to get a good project report made.

Things to keep in mind during this stage are that make sure the report is realistic and can be put to execution as it is. Don't leave any loose ends in your reports.

Look at the cash flows. Look at how much capital will be needed. Understand the percentage profits etc. Is it too low a margin to work for? Think about all of it.

Look at the processes that you will implement for smooth functioning. End to end process and the automation it is going to need etc.

Keep the project report as close as possible to reality and execution.

Let us go to the next step…
Once your project report is ready, you will have two options, either start right away with your investments if required or go to investors or venture capitalists.

If you start and in midway you need funding then too follow all the given steps and you shall succeed in selling your idea successfully as long it is viable commercially.

Fund Raising

Many entrepreneurs and not sales people and that is where they fail initially. They just don't know how to go to market with their products and businesses and how to sell their ideas etc. to others.

First and foremost, remove any inhibitions about sales that you have in your mind. All successful business people are excellent salesmen. They have sold their ideas and products and services to others for years and that is what has brought them wealth and fame.

So if you wish to be successful businessman, it is important to learn to sell.
Don't be shy.
Be bold to go to market with your business and product.
Have total faith in your business idea. If you have even one percent doubt in your mind don't go, or clear your doubt and then go.

Because, it is important to have one hundred percent conviction in your business idea only then others will believe in it.

Make a sales pitch.

Be clear how much investment you are seeking. Against the investment how much percentage shares are you giving to investors.

Or how many years you will need their money and how much interest you will pay. Depends what terms you want, but be clear about it. Keep a room for negotiations. And most importantly don't be stingy. Make a win-win offer. Show them the money.

Once you are ready with the pitch commercials, make a list of investors that you want to target. There are several websites that bring you in contact to angel investors, find them and reach as many as you can.

There are venture capitalists firms who discuss your business plan with potential investors and if shortlisted, arrange your meeting with the investors, meet as many venture capitalists you can.

When you have several options open, you are in a better position to close the deal faster.

Things that investors will be interested in are ROI and valuation of the business after a few years. This is most important for them. If you have not made any plans about valuation of your business then you will need to rework your numbers.

Investors are not interested in how much money they will start making in a year or so. But they are more interested in the valuation of your business after a few years. Your valuation should multiply and that is what they look at. For investors, your pitch should be on valuation. That's the key.

If you are able to do this realistically then you have investor ready to invest.

Valuation will come when you have enough sales in pipeline and you are confident of scaling your business quickly.

If you have done a pilot project with actual numbers that would help you tremendously in closing deal quickly.

So the key here is valuation.

The selling techniques that I have shared in earlier chapters will apply in this case as well as the fundamentals of sales would remain the same.

The investors should see the passion in you for your business, but don't expect them to be passionate about your business. They will only be passionate about their money and valuation, remember this and play it accordingly.

Play to win.

AFTERWORD

I am glad that you have completed this book and I believe that you have already started to use the Sales Process and several Closing Techniques that I have shared with you all.

Come out of your comfort zone and start doing those sales calls that you have been thinking of. It is time for action now. Your presence in the market will decide your success. The more you stay in the market the more sales you will generate.

Use sales management tools that I have shared with you. Get them in place and start monitoring your daily activity. Analyse the things you are doing well and the things that you need to improve upon. Get your number of sales calls up.

Your sales call should be exactly like it has been mentioned in this book. The quality of your sales call will do up considerably with the sales process and other techniques that I have mentioned.

I have attached a practical work book for you. Use blank spaces to plan and write your goals, purpose, product benefits, positioning, different closing statements as per your product etc.

This will help you immensely to close your sales calls faster.

I wish you happy selling and want you to enjoy the experience.

Thank you.

Deepaq V Vartak

SALES SKOOL

Master Sales System

Handbook and Blue Print

By
Deepaq V Vartak

Website: www.salesskool.in , +91 9320220234 What's App/Call

Master Sales System

I am passionate about being in Sales/Business

Beauty Of Sales/Business is

I can write _____

And

I can choose _____

My Own Pay cheque, My time of work

What's Your Purpose of Being in Sales/Business?

I am in Sales For

1.
_____

_____

_____

2.
_____

_____

_____

Make Money For What?

1.
_____

_____

_____

2.
_____

_____

_____

My Commitment

I am willing to invest _____

And _____

That's My Promise To Myself and My Family

Time, Efforts
☐

Master Sales System

Step 1 - Source

Step 2 - Connect

Step 3 - Serve

Step - 1

SOURCING

_____

_____

Prospecting, Planning

☐

Prospecting

Poor Seed, Worst Fruit

_____ Seed, _____ Fruit

If you want Mango stand below a _____ Tree, Not a Papaya Tree..

Similarly If you want High Paying Clients, Do Prospecting In High Class Localities/Business areas
Remember the Power of _____
Other Prospecting Activities…

Good, Great, Mango, Referencing

Planning

Old Saying
If you Fail to _____, you plan to _____

Product information is one of the most important part of the Planning process.

Know Your Product thoroughly.

Know the Competitors Products thoroughly.

Plan your...
Tele-calling For The Day
Sales Calls For The Day
Specific Products For Each Client
Service Calls if any
COI Calls (Centre Of Influence)
Tour Plan for the day/Month
Meeting Agenda For Each Sales Call and outcome

Plan, Fail

Step - 2

Connect
Steps Involved in Connect
Meeting & Greeting
Rapport Building
Strong Opening
Identifying Buying Motive

Before Your Sales Call
Basic Research about the prospective client through…
☐

1.   Right way of Meeting & Greeting

Be _____ about meeting the client

Always have a pleasant _____ while greeting.

Have a _____ handshake

AND NEVER ASK YOUR CLIENT THIS QUESTION

" _____ _____ _____ "

Have a _____ body language

Maintain a decent eye contact (not too heavy nor too avoiding)

Enthusiastic, Smile, Firm, How are you?, Submissive

2. **Rapport Building**

People Buy PEOPLE. Products are incidental

The buyer has to like YOU first, before he decides to do business with YOU.

Common excuse given by Sales Professionals is "They Don't Have Time" to do Rapport Building.
No wonder they end up selling less…
Remove that mental BLOCK…

Start conversation on various topics on a POSITIVE note ONLY
Vacation
Weather
Cars
Sports bikes
Latest news
Sports
Food
New restaurant in client's neighbourhood
His style and choice of clothes, furniture, office ambience etc.
His Friends, colleagues
His watch
His fitness
His staff
Location of his house or office

Strictly avoid topics on Politics, Religion and sexual preferences etc.
☐

3. **Strong Opening**

Your Opening Statement should be a Strong, Catchy and Positive.

Opening statement of your sales call/product presentation decides the flow of you call.

Be creative…

4. **Identifying Buying Motive**

Buying motive is the real reason why customers make a purchase.
Majority of the buying motives can be as below...

Convenience

Performance/Efficiency

Safety Features

Appearance/Aesthetics

Economy

Pride/Pleasure

There can be many more. But these are the major ones.
☐

Step - 3

Serve

If you have done earlier two steps correctly then this final step becomes just a formality.

Steps involved in this Final Step are...

Need Analysis/ Need Creation
Product Presentation
Objection Handling
Closing

Need Analysis/Need Creation

There is always a Need and always a Product available to fulfil that need.

You have to be a good Listener to identify the need of the prospect.
Your tools for Need Identification are Listening & Probing
☐
At what stages can you do Need Identification?
1. During knowing about the client on Social Media/Reference etc.
2. By observing the client's home/office etc.
3. During rapport building/general warm up
4. At times by asking direct questions during Product Presentation (needs experience/practice)
5. Always... just be alert to the buying signals all the time

If you have done your rapport building correctly then the prospect will not hesitate to answer your "Probing Questions" during any stage of the call.
☐

Product Presentation

Be clear about which Product you are going to recommend to your client.

Take a subtle permission before presenting your product

Don't be in a hurry to run through your product presentation. Take your time and do justice to it.

1. Be clear of the product that you must pitch to the prospect
2. Be flexible as per client's needs
3. Don't bombard the prospect with too many products and options.
4. Clearly communicate the Communication Objectives of your product

Today's client is well informed as the information is easily available, so make sure you give 100% genuine information about your product.

Use FABing. This is a game changer.
☐

Objection Handling

Objection is an Opportunity to Sell.

No Objection = ___ _____

Follow The Process…

L_____
A_____
P_____
A_____
C_____

No Sale, Listen, Acknowledge, Probe, Answer, Confirm

The LAPAC Process for Handling Objections

The moment your prospect raises an objection, listen to him carefully.

Acknowledge him by saying 'Thank You Sir' for raising an objection.

If you have any doubts then probe him further with a question or two that why and from where this objection is coming.

Is it coming from past experiences? Is it coming from just listening to somebody?

Or it is just a genuine concern of his?

Once you are clear of the objection and its source, answer it in detail.

Once you have answered the objection, check with the client if he is satisfied with the answer? Have you answered his query correctly?

This is a very simple yet very effective process for handling objections.

Identify the difference between Real and False(Stalling) Objections and deal accordingly.
☐

Closing

Immediately after you handle the objection from the prospect, it's time to go for the _____.

AFTB

If you have followed the complete sales process, then it is your right to Ask For The _____

Golden Rule: "ALWAYS BE CLOSING"

Successful Closing Techniques
1. **Direct Close**

Example- "Would you like to go ahead with this new product that serves your ………, and helps you to……….. "

Close, Business,

2. **The Summary Close**

Example- "Well Sir, this is the product that matches your requirements (narrate the requirement) and also fits in your budget. How about buying one today?"

3. **Third Party Close**

Example- "Sir, this is just to share with you, Mr……….. in your neighbourhood had similar inhibitions about trying our new range, but after using it he totally satisfied and now a regular customer of ours. Let us start with a initial order and see how you feel about it."

☐

4. **Trial Basis Close**

Example- "Well Sir, I can see you still have little inhibitions about using our range....., hence to help you to arrive at a decision, you can buy a trial pack with us. And once you are satisfied, you can place a regular order with us."

5. **The Alternative Option**

Example- "Sir, which one would you like to buy? M500 or M750? Both will serve your purpose".

In this method you are not giving any other option to the prospect. This is very assertive closing.

☐

6.   **The Assumptive Close**

Example- "Sir, considering your need and usage, I suggest you to go for this version….."

Now, after you have used any of these closing techniques, there are only three possible outcomes

Yes, I will buy it now.

No. I don't want to but now/I don't need it now.

Let me think.

In case of 'YES', just take out your order form and start filling and ask for the cheque number or payment method. Ask for references.

In case of 'NO', Probe further.

In case of 'LET ME THINK' there is one more final closing technique called;

7. The Build Up Close Or Method Of Continued Affirmation

Immediately say "Sir thank you for giving a thought to my product/......."

☐

"Sir, just to sum it up, you will agree that this suits your need of ...." Right sir?

"My product benefits of …….. & ……. Offer you……..", right sir?

"In that case, if this fulfils your need and also offers you benefits as good as these, then what's stopping you from taking a decision? Please let me know so that I can help."

If the prospect opens up and talks about limited finances, you know how to nail it. Either show your value proposition or offer payment plan and close the deal.

I am sharing three more powerful closing techniques, but I add a word of caution to it. Please use these techniques only if you are confident and totally in control of your sales call.

I have used these very often and my closing ration with these techniques has been close to 100%. That tells you how powerful these are.

☐

8. Half Nelson Technique

When to use:

When a prospect is showing no interest/trust in your product or services.

When he says "I have seen many such products. They don't work etc."

How to use this:

"Sir, thank you for sharing your concern. Well if I show/prove it to you that my product has got all the features and benefits that you are looking at, gives value for money, and suits your exact needs, then in that case WILL YOU BUY MY PRODUCT TODAY?"

Rest is just a formality as you are confident of doing a strong presentation and after objection handling, sign him up.

☐

Other powerful Closing Technique is:

9. BULL's EYE

When to use:

Can be used before you begin your sales presentation. During rapport building if you have managed to get important information about what your prospect is looking for, then use this technique.

"Sir, if I am not mistaken, ... is this what you are looking for in a product?"

You have to hit the bull's eye in terms of his needs/ requirement/ wants.

If you manage to do that, he will jump out of his seat and hold your hand and say, yes man, you are right, this is exactly what I am looking for, do you have one?

Then position your product benefits accordingly and close it.

☐

10. Crawl-back Close

WARNING: This technique is to be used only when over a period of time you have done everything in your control and you have tried all the closing techniques at various points and you have not got the desired result. Or else if you use this technique too early, you will be taken as a week person. So use this technique judiciously.

This technique is used in cases where you have been trying hard to convert a Super Smart Customer but he has not yet given you any business. There is a need, you have the product, you have done everything in your control yet failed to get business.

Mostly in cases where there is a Big Distributor, an Opinion Leader, Top COI (centre of influence), etc.

What You Say- "Sir, I need your guidance today. I will not speak to you about business today. But I want your invaluable feedback."

Sir, you are aware that I have done everything in my capacity to convince you to ....

I know you have the potential/need. I know I have the products range that matches your/your customers' needs. But still I have failed to convince you. I request you to help me in understanding what mistake I am doing so that in future I will learn to serve Top Distributor/ etc. etc. like you... Have I ever hurt you in any way?

Please tell me sir...

Invariably he will share the reason and that's your time to CRAWL-BACK in to close the sales call...

Thank him for sharing the reason and go for the close.

☐

FABing

F_____
A_____
B_____

Don't sell just Features, learn to sell Benefits. Benefits are visible.

Prospects _____ to benefits

Features, Advantages, Benefits, Relate

☐
Sales Management

_____ is your best friend

Inspect what you expect

Remember, Data Speaks…

Learn to fill the data sheets so that your MIS speaks truth to you and guides you.

Some of the must have MIS reports (updated)
1. Daily/Weekly/Monthly Call Reports
2. Business figures data
3. Client data – visit/business
4. Lead generation activity reports

MIS

Sales Business Review Mechanism

Reviews help you to be on track
If you are doing good you Must know why you are doing good and if you are doing bad, you Must know why you are doing bad.

Mid-month review
To be done in the mid of the month
Business achievement versus targets to be analysed
If above target, then look to aver achieve
If falling short, make plans to complete your targets as decided at the beginning of the month
Focus on Data

Monthly review
To be done at the beginning of the month
To look back at last month figures and then plan for current month figures

Set Milestones
Appreciate performers
Support non-performers by doing Joint filed calls, trainings etc. instil confidence in them

Focus on Data. No stories.

☐
Feedback

Giving and receiving feedback is an art.

Focus on constructive feedback

While giving feedback, speak about the positives first. Tell the person what are his strengths and the things that he is doing well.

Then go to the area of improvement section. Tell him things that he needs to do well and if he masters those things then how he will add value to himself and his work.

Be genuine and look to add value to the person without hurting his/her feelings.

First gain confidence and respect before giving the feedback.

You must also learn to seek and accept feedback from your superiors and well-wishers.

☐

Listening Skills

We spend 70% of our time in communicating with others. Out of this 70%

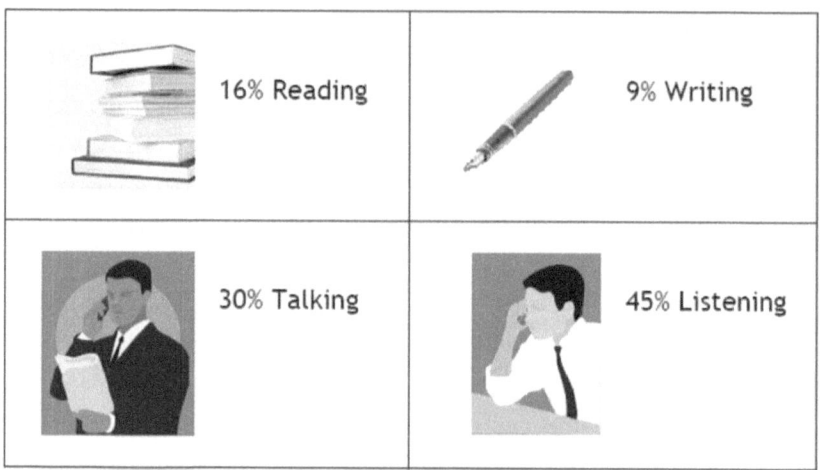

Understand the importance of "Listening".

Your sales call has to be a dialogue, not a monologue.
☐
When you listen to the customer
He feels...
Recognized and remembered
Valued
Appreciated
Respected
Understood
Comfortable about his want or need

Selling by Listening...

Great salespeople are great listeners.
The most critical communication skill for anyone in the business world is effective listening.

People don't buy what you wish to sell. They buy what they need.
Selling is not happening when you are talking.
Selling is happening when your prospect is talking.
☐

Traits Of A Good Listener
Being non-evaluative
Eye Contact
Positive Body Language
Positive Verbal Signal
Positive Facial Expression
Asks Good/Right Questions
Inviting further contributions
80-20 Rule

Listening is the most powerful form of acknowledgment

...a way of saying to your customer, "YOU ARE IMPORTANT."
☐

Probing Skills

Telling isn't Selling

Asking is ... Most crucial for consultative selling.

Important Rule of Probing : Always ask Questions in a Learning mode

Common Types Of Questions in Probing
Open Ended Questions
Close Ended Questions
Fact Finding Questions
Leading Questions
Reflective Questions
Narrowing (E.S.P.) Questions

Open Ended Questions start with..

What
When
Who
Where
How
Why (Use with caution)

Examples:
"Are there typically no symptoms in the early stages of bone loss. How do you overcome the problem of early detection Sir?"

"In the treatment of Osteoporosis, managing increased need of calcium in elders is a real problem what is your opinion Sir?"
☐

Close Ended Questions
Start with...
Did
Can
Was
Where
Is
Do/Does

Examples:
"Do obese women have greater risk of infertility?"

"Do your clients ask you for Mutual Funds with names, or they ask for your suggestions?"
☐

Fact Finding Questions are used to...

Get behind the previous answer
Find more details
Need clarification
Want to prevent misunderstanding

Examples:
"Sir, what's the real reason that's stopping you from suggesting products to your clients"

"Sir, what age group clients would be ideal to by our Mutual Funds?

"As per you, which is the best Mutual Fund in the market?"
☐

Narrowing (E.S.P.) Questions

Exactly
Specifically
Precisely
☐

Leading Questions

Want to lead the client in a direction of your choice..?
These are good for getting answers you want coming from the customer's mouth himself!!!

Technique for asking leading questions...
1. Show personal preference
2. Phrase questions to get a "YES"
3. Assume something as fact without questioning it
☐

Reflective Questions

Reflect back to the Customer's answer and leads to a further question
Demonstrate active listening
"You mentioned that ....   In what way..........
..........?"